BEST OF THE SUPER BOWL

SUPER BOWL RECORD SETTERS

BY DAVID J. CLARKE

SportsZone

An Imprint of Abdo Publishing
abdobooks.com

abdobooks.com

Published by Abdo Publishing, a division of ABDO, PO Box 398166, Minneapolis, Minnesota 55439.

Printed in the United States of America, North Mankato, Minnesota.
102024
012025

THIS BOOK CONTAINS RECYCLED MATERIALS

Cover Photos: David Madison/Getty Images Sport/Getty Images (left); Lutz Bongarts/Bongarts/Getty Images (middle); Focus On Sport/Getty Images (right)
Interior Photos: Focus On Sport/Getty Images Sport/Getty Images, 4, 27; Rob Brown/Getty Images Sport/Getty Images, 6; Al Messerschmidt Archive/AP Images, 9; AFP/Getty Images, 11; Mike Ehrmann/Getty Images Sport/Getty Images, 13; Tony Tomsic/AP Images, 14, 18, 20; Elsa/Getty Images Sport/Getty Images, 17; Marcio J. Sanchez/AP Images, 23; Focus On Sport/Getty Images, 24, 31; Stephen Dunn/Allsport/Getty Images Sport/Getty Images, 28; Rick Stewart/Allsport/Getty Images Sport/Getty Images, 30; Rob Carr/Getty Images Sport/Getty Images, 33; James Flores/Getty Images Sport/Getty Images, 34; Richard Stagg/Getty Images Sport/Getty Images, 37; Rich Kane/Icon SMI/Corbis/Icon Sportswire/Getty Images, 38; Michael Zagaris/Getty Images Sport/Getty Images, 41; Lynne Sladky/AP Images, 43; Kathryn Riley/AP Images, 44; Brian Bahr/Getty Images Sport/Getty Images, 45

Editor: Charlie Beattie
Series Designer: Jake Slavik

Library of Congress Control Number: 2024938339

Publisher's Cataloging-in-Publication Data

Names: Clarke, David J., author.
Title: Super Bowl record setters / by David J. Clarke
Description: Minneapolis, Minnesota: ABDO Publishing, 2025 | Series: Best of the Super Bowl | Includes online resources and index.
Identifiers: ISBN 9781098295431 (lib. bdg.) | ISBN 9798384916437 (ebook)
Subjects: LCSH: Super Bowl--Records--Juvenile literature. | Football--Records--Juvenile literature. | American football--Juvenile literature. | National Football League--Juvenile literature. | Sports records--Juvenile literature. | Football--United States--History--Juvenile literature.
Classification: DDC 796.332648--dc23

TABLE OF CONTENTS

CHAPTER ONE

OFFENSIVE EXPLOSIONS

Terry Bradshaw rewrote the Super Bowl record book on January 21, 1979. The strong-armed Pittsburgh Steelers' quarterback used long bombs to become the first 300-yard passer in the game's history. He also became the first quarterback to throw four touchdown passes in a Super Bowl. And, most importantly, Bradshaw's performance in Super Bowl XIII helped the Steelers hold off the Dallas Cowboys to win the game for a record-setting third time.

That offensive explosion turned a lot of heads back in 1979. Through the years, Super Bowl quarterbacks have consistently raised the level, smashing the game's records over and over again. Today, Bradshaw's performance wouldn't even crack the top 10 for

Terry Bradshaw completed 49 passes in four Super Bowl appearances, including nine touchdowns.

Phil Simms, *left*, played for the New York Giants from 1979 to 1993.

Super Bowl passing yards. And several quarterbacks have matched or surpassed Bradshaw's four-touchdown performance.

Entering Super Bowl XXI in January 1987, most of the quarterback focus was on superstar John Elway of the Denver Broncos. The New York Giants' Phil Simms, on the other hand, was merely a steady starter. He had played for the Giants for eight years. Many fans of the team wondered whether he was good enough to win a title. But Simms threw five touchdown passes and no interceptions in the Giants' two National Football Conference (NFC) playoff games. Against the Broncos, he was nearly flawless.

Simms came out firing in the first quarter. On New York's first drive, he was a perfect 6-of-6. His last pass was a six-yard touchdown strike to tight end Zeke Mowatt.

Despite that strong opening, the Giants trailed 10–9 at halftime. Simms was a solid 12-of-15 throwing for 103 yards and a touchdown. But in the second half, the 31-year-old was perfect. Simms completed all 10 of his passes. Even when tight end Mark Bavaro had a Simms pass bounce off his hands, receiver Phil McConkey caught the deflection for a touchdown. The Giants rolled to a 39–20 victory. Simms was named the Most Valuable Player (MVP) after completing 88 percent of his passes on the day. At the time, he was the only quarterback to ever top 80 percent in a Super Bowl game. Bradshaw, for comparison, completed only 56.1 percent of his passes in Super Bowl XIII.

A QUARTER TO REMEMBER

Like the Giants a year earlier, Washington started the second quarter of Super Bowl XXII trailing the Broncos. This time Denver led 10–0. But that was about to change in a big way.

Entering the game, no team had ever scored more than 21 points in a single Super Bowl quarter. And no team had scored more than 28 in a single half. But Washington exploded in the second quarter against the Broncos. On the team's first play, quarterback Doug Williams tossed an 80-yard touchdown pass to wide receiver Ricky Sanders. On its own, that play put Washington in the record books. It tied the record for the longest pass in Super Bowl history at the time. And Washington was far from done.

Just over a minute later, Washington took over at its own 36-yard line. Five plays later, Williams hit receiver Gary Clark on a 27-yard toss. Washington took a 14–10 lead.

Washington got the ball back with just over seven minutes left in the quarter. Once again, the team struck quickly. On the second play of the drive, running back Timmy Smith raced 58 yards down the right sideline for another score. Smith was on his way to his own Super Bowl record of 204 rushing yards in the game. The touchdown put Washington up 21–10.

Less than three minutes later, Williams threw another bomb to Sanders. This 50-yarder put Washington's offense in the record

GANNON'S BAD DAY

Not all Super Bowl records are ones players want to remember. Rich Gannon of the Oakland Raiders was the 2002 NFL MVP. Following that season, he entered Super Bowl XXXVII with big expectations. But when the game was over, the 38-year-old quarterback had thrown a Super Bowl–record five interceptions to the Tampa Bay Buccaneers. To make matters worse, Tampa Bay brought three of them back for touchdowns. That was also a record.

Timmy Smith rushed for two touchdowns in Super Bowl XXII after not scoring at all during the 1987 regular season.

books for the most points in a quarter. Williams completed the ambush with 1:11 left in the half. He threw an eight-yard scoring toss to tight end Clint Didier. Denver never recovered from Washington's monster 15 minutes. The final score of the game was 42–10.

TWICE THE RICE

Jerry Rice of the San Francisco 49ers was already in the Super Bowl record books by the time he took the field in Super Bowl XXIV in January 1990. A year earlier, he had caught 11 passes from quarterback Joe Montana for 216 yards. The pair led San Francisco to a 20–16 win over the Cincinnati Bengals.

This time, Rice and Montana were squaring off against Denver. And they went to the air right away. Less than five minutes into the game, Rice cut across the middle and caught a pass at the Broncos' 8-yard line. He was immediately crunched by Denver safety Steve Atwater. But Rice bounced off the defender and strolled into the end zone with his arms held high.

Later in the first half, Rice caught a 38-yard touchdown pass from Montana. That made him the seventh player to ever catch multiple touchdowns in the same Super Bowl. No one had ever caught three.

Rice became the first just minutes into the second half. With 12:34 left in the third quarter, Montana flung a 28-yard pass to the 49ers' star receiver. This time Rice was belted by Denver's other safety, Dennis Smith. But Rice held on for his record-setting touchdown. San Francisco won the game 55–10.

Exactly five years and one day later, Rice was back in the Super Bowl. But this time he had a different quarterback in lefty Steve Young. But facing the San Diego Chargers in Super Bowl XXIX, Rice's performance didn't change.

On the third play of the game, Young gunned a ball to a sprinting Rice down the middle. The receiver outraced two defensive backs to the end zone. That play set the tone for a 49–26 blowout win. As Young threw a Super Bowl–record six touchdown passes, two more went to Rice. That gave Rice two Super Bowls with three touchdown catches. Thirty years later, no other receiver had ever achieved that even once.

Jerry Rice finished his career with 589 yards and eight touchdown receptions in four Super Bowls.

THE GOAT

Quarterback Tom Brady holds the record for most Super Bowl appearances with 10. So it isn't surprising that Brady also holds most of the game's passing records. What truly separates Brady is how far he is beyond the competition.

At the time of his retirement, Brady's 421 Super Bowl passing attempts were nearly 300 more than Peyton Manning's, who was in second place. Likewise, Brady had completed 277 passes to Manning's 103. Brady's 3,039 passing yards were nearly triple Kurt Warner's second place total of 1,156.

Brady entered Super Bowl XLIX in February 2015 with nine career Super Bowl touchdowns. With 7:55 left in the fourth quarter, he hit receiver Danny Amendola on a four-yard bullet. It was Brady's third of four touchdown passes of the game. It also surpassed Montana's old record of 11. Brady played in four more Super Bowls after that game, throwing eight scores along the way.

Brady also retired as the only quarterback to throw for more than 500 yards, complete more than 40 passes, and attempt more than 60 throws in a Super Bowl game. But the most impressive statistic of Brady's legendary career is his seven wins. No other player has even appeared in that many Super Bowls. At the time of Brady's retirement, no NFL franchise had either.

Tom Brady is one of four players to have appeared in the Super Bowl in three different decades. He is the only player to win the game in all three.

CHAPTER TWO

ENDURING PERFORMANCES

Most teams that reach the Super Bowl feature strong groups on both sides of the ball. With so much talent on the field, it can be tough to dominate an opponent. But a few times throughout the history of the game, a team has done just that.

The Dallas Cowboys reached Super Bowl VI in January 1972 on the strength of their celebrated "Doomsday Defense." Five members of the standout unit eventually reached the Pro Football Hall of Fame. And on that Sunday, the Cowboys crushed the Miami Dolphins.

Miami featured a strong ground attack led by running backs Larry Csonka and Jim Kiick. But the Cowboys held the pair to 40 yards apiece on the ground. Dolphins quarterback Bob Griese didn't fare

Dallas Cowboys defensive lineman Bob Lilly had two tackles and one sack against the Miami Dolphins in Super Bowl VI after the 1971 season.

much better. He completed 12-of-23 passes for only 134 yards and was intercepted once.

One play nicely summed up Miami's day against the Doomsday Defense. Late in the first quarter, Griese dropped back to pass from the Miami 38-yard line. Dallas linemen Larry Cole and Bob Lilly immediately set off after him. Instead of going down, Griese tried to keep the play alive. He kept backing up until Cole finally brought him down at the 9-yard line for a 29-yard loss. In the end, the Dolphins gained only 185 yards in a 24–3 defeat. They also became the first team in Super Bowl history that failed to score a touchdown in the game.

It took 48 years for another team to be held out of the end zone in Super Bowl play. The Los Angeles Rams had scored 527 points during the 2018 regular season. But in the Super Bowl, they faced the New England Patriots and their masterful defensive coach, Bill Belichick. The Pats' defense clamped down on Rams quarterback Jared Goff and held the Rams to only three points. Goff was sacked four times.

The Patriots didn't fare much better, however. Los Angeles held New England quarterback Tom Brady down. It was the only time in Brady's 10 Super Bowl appearances that he failed to throw a touchdown pass. New England running back Sony Michel scored the game's only touchdown. The 13–3 Patriots win was the lowest scoring Super Bowl in history.

Los Angeles Rams quarterback Jared Goff is smothered by a pair of New England Patriots defenders in Super Bowl LIII after the 2019 season.

STEEL CURTAIN

Super Bowl IX in January 1975 was set to be a defensive struggle. The Pittsburgh Steelers' "Steel Curtain" and the Minnesota Vikings' "Purple People Eaters" both devoured opposing offenses. Sure enough, the game was a low-scoring grind.

The only points of the first half came on a piece of Super Bowl history. With 7:34 left in the second quarter, Minnesota lined up for a

Jack Lambert (58) and the Pittsburgh Steelers held Minnesota to just 17 yards rushing on 21 carries in Super Bowl IX on January 12, 1975.

second-and-7 play at its own 10. Vikings quarterback Fran Tarkenton fumbled a handoff and had to go back into the end zone to pick it up. Tarkenton fell on the ball and was touched down by Pittsburgh defensive end Dwight White. It was the first safety ever recorded in a Super Bowl.

Life wasn't much easier for Pittsburgh's offense. The Steelers kept forcing their way forward, though. Running back Franco Harris ultimately managed 158 rushing yards on 34 carries. Both were

Super Bowl records at the time. He added a nine-yard touchdown run in the third quarter to make it 9–0. Quarterback Terry Bradshaw added a short touchdown pass to receiver Larry Brown in the fourth quarter.

Meanwhile, Pittsburgh's defense never let up, keeping Minnesota to a Super Bowl-low 119 yards of offense. And the Steel Curtain could have had the game's first shutout if it weren't for a special teams mistake. With 11:02 left in the game, Vikings linebacker Matt Blair blocked a punt inside the Pittsburgh 10-yard line. Minnesota defensive back Terry Brown recovered in the end zone. The Vikings missed the extra point, but Pittsburgh had to settle for a 16–6 win. Nearly 50 years later, still no team had been shut out in a Super Bowl.

SPECIAL TEAMS ACES

A good kicking game can often mean the difference between winning and losing. In Super Bowl II after the 1967 season, Green Bay kicker Don Chandler kicked four field goals in a 33–14 win. That established a record that more than 50 years later has been matched but never broken.

Green Bay would have still beaten the Oakland Raiders without Chandler's accurate boots. However, the same cannot be said for Ray Wersching and the San Francisco 49ers in Super Bowl XVI on January 24, 1982. Wersching matched Chandler's record with boots of 22, 26, 40, and 23 yards. He also added two extra points. The 49ers

Don Chandler (34) of the Green Bay Packers boots one of his four field goals in Super Bowl II after the 1967 season.

needed every one of Wersching's 14 points to defeat the Cincinnati Bengals 26–21.

In February 2024, Harrison Butker of the Kansas City Chiefs became the third kicker to reach four field goals in a Super Bowl. Butker entered the game having gone 5-of-6 in three previous Super Bowls. Perhaps his most memorable performance had come after the 2022 season in Super Bowl LVII. His clutch game-winner with seconds remaining sent the Chiefs past the Philadelphia Eagles 38–35. His 4-of-4 performance against the 49ers the next year in Super Bowl LVIII cemented Butker as the most accomplished kicker in Super Bowl history.

Butker began his Super Bowl LVIII performance by hitting a routine 28-yard attempt with 20 seconds left in the first half. With 5:01 left in the third quarter, he blasted a 57-yarder through the uprights. That set a new Super Bowl record for longest field goal.

Butker hit from 24 yards out to tie the score 16–16 with 5:46 left in

MOODY'S MOMENT

In the first quarter of Super Bowl LVIII in February 2024, San Francisco 49ers kicker Jake Moody knocked in a 55-yard field goal. That broke the record of 54 set by Steve Christie of the Buffalo Bills in Super Bowl XXVIII in January 1994. While Christie's record lasted nearly three decades, Moody's lasted only two quarters. Kansas City Chiefs kicker Harrison Butker's 57-yarder topped the mark in the third quarter of the same game.

the game. The kick set another record. His eighth career made attempt moved Butker past Adam Vinatieri and Stephen Gostkowski for the most in Super Bowl history.

Butker capped off his record-smashing day by tying the game 19–19 on a 29-yarder with three seconds left in regulation. The Chiefs eventually won 25–22 in overtime. That meant a third Super Bowl ring to go along with his incredible statistics. And Butker was still just 28 years old.

Harrison Butker (7) kicks the game-winning field goal against the Philadelphia Eagles in Super Bowl LVII on February 12, 2023.

58
58

CHAPTER THREE

BIGGEST, BEST, AND WORST

Many Super Bowls have been amazing games. Of the first 58 Super Bowls, 23 were decided by a touchdown or less. Two went to overtime, and four were decided by field goals—either missed or made—in the final minute.

However, a few Super Bowls turned into super blowouts. The Green Bay Packers beat the Kansas City Chiefs 35–10 in Super Bowl I after the 1966 season. A year later, Green Bay rocked the Oakland Raiders 33–14.

Some of the most lopsided games took place in the 1980s and early 1990s. During that time, the NFC won 13 straight Super Bowls. Few of them were close games. One of the biggest romps was

Chicago Bears linebacker Wilber Marshall runs with the ball after recovering a fumble against the New England Patriots in Super Bowl XX after the 1985 season.

Super Bowl XX. During that 1985 season, the Chicago Bears finished 15–1. The team's strength was its "46" defense. It was a scheme filled with creative blitzes designed by innovative defensive coordinator Buddy Ryan. Few teams stood a chance against Chicago. That included the underdog New England Patriots in the Super Bowl.

The Bears mauled New England quarterbacks Steve Grogan and Tony Eason for seven sacks. They intercepted Grogan twice. Eason lost a fumble.

The final score was Chicago 46, New England 10. Not surprisingly, the MVP of the game was a Chicago defensive star. Bears defensive end Richard Dent recorded 1 1/2 sacks and forced two fumbles in the game.

Four years later, the San Francisco 49ers faced the Denver Broncos in Super Bowl XXIV. Both teams had reached the big game multiple times during the 1980s, but with different results. San Francisco had won it three times. Denver had been blown out in both Super Bowl XXI in January 1987 and Super Bowl XXII a year later.

Super Bowl XXIV was played on January 28, 1990. But the new year didn't change either team's fortunes. Denver struggled to get anything going on offense. Star quarterback John Elway completed only 10-of-26 passes and was intercepted twice. On the other side, Joe Montana won his then-record third Super Bowl MVP Award. He threw five touchdown passes against the Broncos, which was also a record at the time. The final score was 55–10. More than three

In 2017, NFL.com voted Super Bowl XXIV as the least entertaining of all time.

Bills fans suffered through heartbreak at four consecutive Super Bowls in the early 1990s.

decades later, the 45-point margin of victory was still the largest in the game's history.

BUFFALO'S BAD YEARS

The Broncos' heavy loss in Super Bowl XXIV was the franchise's fourth appearance without a win. That tied a record set by the Minnesota

Vikings in the 1960s and 1970s. But the next year, a new team came along to start a heartbreaking Super Bowl streak.

The Buffalo Bills were one of the most exciting teams in the NFL in the early 1990s. Their no-huddle "K-Gun" offense moved the ball quickly and rolled up high scores. After the 1990 season, coach Marv Levy's team reached its first Super Bowl. The Bills faced off with the New York Giants in Super Bowl XXV. But Giants defensive coordinator Bill Belichick installed a blitzing game plan that slowed down the K-Gun. Despite that, the Bills still had a chance to win. But kicker Scott Norwood missed a 47-yard field goal attempt in the final seconds of Buffalo's 20–19 defeat.

A year later, the Bills were back for Super Bowl XXVI. Facing Washington, Buffalo turned the ball over five times. The Bills fell behind 24–0 and never recovered. Washington won 37–24.

The Bills once again strolled through the American Football Conference (AFC) in 1992. But mistakes got the best of Buffalo once again in the Super Bowl. The Dallas Cowboys forced a Super Bowl–record nine turnovers. The game was close at halftime, but Dallas rolled in the second half. The final was one of the worst blowouts in the game's history as Dallas won 52–17.

The same two teams met in Super Bowl XXVIII in January 1994. This time, Buffalo held a 13–6 lead at halftime. But the Bills couldn't keep up with the Cowboys in the final two quarters. The final was 30–13 in Dallas's favor.

Buffalo Bills running back Thurman Thomas hangs his head on the sidelines after the Bills' fourth straight Super Bowl loss.

For years after the Bills' losses, the team was ridiculed for falling short on football's biggest stage. Over time, however, Buffalo's achievement has been given more credit. In the years that followed, both Denver and New England established a new high mark with five Super Bowl losses. Meanwhile, another way to look at Buffalo's streak is that the Bills are also the only team to ever reach the Super Bowl in four straight years.

SUPER SHOOTOUT

During the 2017 NFL season, the Patriots and Philadelphia Eagles each averaged 28.6 points per game. That trailed only the Los Angeles Rams for the highest scoring offense in the league. So when the Eagles and Patriots met in Super Bowl LII, an offensive game was expected.

The shootout went beyond anyone's wildest dreams. Philadelphia won the game 41–33. The 74 combined points fell just one shy of a Super Bowl record. Just about every other offensive number from Super Bowl LII went into the record books, though. The teams tied the record for most first downs in a

SHULA STAYS GROUNDED

In the 1970s, coach Don Shula's teams were known for running the ball. His Miami Dolphins won back-to-back championships in the 1972 and 1973 seasons. Miami completed just eight passes in a 14–7 win over Washington in Super Bowl VII. Dolphins quarterback Bob Griese went 6-of-7 passing in a 24–7 victory over the Minnesota Vikings the next year. A decade later, Miami fell 27–17 to Washington in Super Bowl XVII. Two Dolphins quarterbacks broke Griese's record in that game by combining for only four completions.

game with 54. There was only one punt in the game, which was also a record. New England's 613 yards of total offense was the most of any team in Super Bowl history. And together, Philadelphia and New England had put up 1,151 total yards. That was not just a Super Bowl record. It was the highest combined total in any NFL game, regular season or playoffs.

Amazingly, the most offensive of Super Bowls turned on a great defensive play. With 2:16 left, the Eagles led 38–33. On second-and-2 from his own 33, Patriots quarterback Tom Brady was taken down by the Eagles' Brandon Graham. It was the game's only sack. Making matters even worse for the Patriots, Brady fumbled, and Philadelphia defensive end Derek Barnett recovered. Four plays later, Eagles kicker Jake Elliott capped off the incredible night with a 46-yard field goal. Though the Patriots tried to mount a final drive, it came up short. Philadelphia won 41–33 after Brady's last-second Hail Mary pass fell incomplete.

Philadelphia Eagles tight end Zach Ertz, *left*, runs over New England Patriots safety Devin McCourty to score the winning touchdown in Super Bowl LII after the 2017 season.

CHAPTER FOUR

SUPER BOWL FIRSTS

Herb Adderley of the Green Bay Packers was a Hall of Fame cornerback in his career. He was also the first player to ever get his hands on the ball in a Super Bowl. At the start of Super Bowl I on January 15, 1967, Adderley received the opening kickoff from the Kansas City Chiefs and returned it 20 yards.

With the game being new, many super "firsts" were established that day. The Chiefs took the first penalty when they were called for a delay of game on their first drive. Later in the first quarter, Green Bay quarterback Bart Starr hit receiver Max McGee for the Super Bowl's first touchdown. Kansas City kicker Mike Mercer knocked in the first field goal with 1:25 left in the first half.

A year later, Adderley was involved in another Super Bowl first. With just under 12 minutes left in Super Bowl II, his Packers were

Willie Mitchell, *right*, of the Kansas City Chiefs tries to tackle receiver Max McGee of the Green Bay Packers during Super Bowl I on January 15, 1967.

leading the Oakland Raiders 26–7. Oakland quarterback Daryle Lamonica tried to throw a pass to the right side of the field for receiver Fred Biletnikoff. Adderley swooped in and picked it off at the Packers' 40-yard line. He then raced the other way. Lamonica had a chance to bring Adderley down at the Oakland 20. But Adderley put on a strong juke and raced to the end zone. It was the first defensive touchdown in Super Bowl history. There would not be another one until Super Bowl XI in January 1977.

WINNING WHILE LOSING

Adderley didn't win any awards for his Super Bowl II performance. But in Super Bowl V, Dallas Cowboys linebacker Chuck Howley was named the game's MVP. He intercepted two passes and recovered a Baltimore Colts fumble. Howley was the first defensive player to win the award.

There was only one problem for the Dallas linebacker. The Cowboys didn't win the game. Baltimore emerged victorious on a late field goal for a 16–13 final. Howley became the first MVP from a losing team. More than 50 years after that strange feat, he was still the only player in that category.

RETURN TO GREATNESS

On the first play of the second half in Super Bowl XLVIII on February 2, 2014, Seattle Seahawks receiver Percy Harvin received a kickoff at his

Chuck Howley played for the Dallas Cowboys from 1961 to 1973.

Percy Harvin (11) breaks a tackle on his way to the end zone during Super Bowl XLVIII in February 2014.

own 13-yard line. The speedster blasted up the middle and evaded two tackles on his way to the end zone. It was one of many highlights of Seattle's 43–8 blowout win over the Denver Broncos.

It was also the 10th kickoff returned for a score in the history of the Super Bowl. Most of them had come since the mid-1990s. Between Super Bowl XXIX in January 1995 and Super Bowl XXXV in January 2001, there were five kick returns for scores. Both the Baltimore Ravens and the New York Giants returned kickoffs for touchdowns in Super Bowl XXXV. The scores even came on back-to-back plays.

However, the game's early years featured no such highlights. It took a while for any player to run back a kickoff for a touchdown in Super Bowl play. Late in the second quarter of Super Bowl XVII after the 1982 season, Washington running back Alvin Garrett scored on a four-yard rush. The play tied his team with Miami 10–10.

Dolphins return man Fulton Walker grabbed Mark Moseley's kickoff at the 2-yard line. He sprinted all the way across the field before cutting and exploding through a hole. No Washington player could get close to Walker as he raced 98 yards for his historic return. In the end, however, the play didn't help Miami. The Dolphins failed to score for the rest of the game. Washington rallied for a 27–17 victory.

PUNT RETURNS

While there have been several kickoff returns for touchdowns in Super Bowls, no player has returned a punt for a touchdown. Kansas City Chiefs receiver Kadarius Toney came the closest. In Super Bowl LVII after the 2022 season, Toney brought a Philadelphia Eagles punt back a Super Bowl–record 65 yards early in the fourth quarter. Eagles punter Arryn Siposs saved a touchdown by forcing Toney out of bounds at the Philadelphia 5-yard line. Kansas City scored a touchdown three plays later.

BREAKING BARRIERS

Like athletes in other sports, Black football players and coaches experienced discrimination for many years. NFL owners refused to sign Black players for nearly two decades until the sport's color barrier was broken in 1946. But for decades after that moment, many NFL coaches and owners still did not field Black quarterbacks. A racist stereotype existed in football that said Black players did not have the mental abilities for such a tough position.

Doug Williams was one of the few Black NFL quarterbacks in the late 1970s. But he spent the 1980s bouncing between the NFL and a rival league called the United States Football League. Williams signed with Washington before the 1986 season to be the backup. But just before the playoffs in 1987, head coach Joe Gibbs promoted Williams to starter. Williams responded by leading the team to two wins. That set Washington up for a matchup with the Denver Broncos in Super Bowl XXII. And Williams was ready to make history.

Williams didn't just show up for Super Bowl XXII. He played the game of his life. The 32-year-old threw for 340 yards and four touchdowns. Three of them came in Washington's record-setting 35-point second quarter. After the game, Williams was named MVP.

Williams's performance helped open the door for other Black quarterbacks. Since his win, more and more players of color have led teams. In 2022, 68 quarterbacks started at least one NFL game. Twenty-one were Black. After the season, Patrick Mahomes and the Chiefs faced Jalen Hurts and the Philadelphia Eagles in Super Bowl LVII. It marked the first time that both Super Bowl starters were Black.

Doug Williams matched his career high with four touchdowns in Super Bowl XXII in January 1988. He reached that total twice in 88 career regular-season games.

Tony Dungy was a star quarterback in college at the University of Minnesota. But when he got to the NFL in 1977, he suffered the same fate as many Black college quarterbacks. The Pittsburgh Steelers moved him to defensive back. Dungy played three years in the NFL and won one Super Bowl with the Steelers. After his career was over in 1980, he turned to coaching.

Black coaches suffered through the same struggle as Black quarterbacks. Fritz Pollard was the head coach of the Akron Pros, an early NFL team, in 1921. But the second Black head coach in the NFL wasn't hired until 68 years later. Art Shell took charge of the Los Angeles Raiders in 1988. When Dungy was hired by the Tampa Bay Buccaneers in 1996, he was just the fifth Black head coach in league history.

Dungy didn't reach the Super Bowl with the Buccaneers. But he guided the Indianapolis Colts to Super Bowl XLI in February 2007 against the Chicago Bears. He would have been alone as the first Black coach to reach the Super Bowl if it weren't for the man on the other sideline. The Bears were coached by Dungy's former assistant Lovie Smith. The two men were incredibly close friends who were thrilled to be making history together.

In a rain-soaked game in Miami, Dungy's Colts won 29–17. Afterward, Dungy told the media, "I tell you what, I'm proud to be representing African-American coaches, to be the first African-American coach to win this. It means an awful lot to our country."

Tony Dungy is carried off the field by his assistants after his Indianapolis Colts defeated the Chicago Bears in Super Bowl XLI on February 4, 2007.

HONORABLE MENTIONS

JOE VERSATILE

Five head coaches have won at least three Super Bowls. But only one has done it with more than one quarterback. Washington's Joe Gibbs won Super Bowl XVII in January 1983 with Joe Theismann. He then coached Doug Williams to victory in Super Bowl XXII after the 1987 season. Finally, Gibbs won Super Bowl XXVI in January 1992, with Mark Rypien as his starter.

THE ROOKIE

Only one coach has won the Super Bowl in his rookie season as the head man. Don McCafferty led the Baltimore Colts to a 16–13 win against the Dallas Cowboys in January 1971. McCafferty had only taken over before the season when the legendary Don Shula left Baltimore for the Miami Dolphins. McCafferty left the team two seasons later, having not reached the Super Bowl again.

BROTHER VS. BROTHER

Super Bowl LVII was a family affair. Travis Kelce caught six passes for 81 yards and a touchdown as a tight end for the Kansas City Chiefs. His older brother Jason started at center for the Philadelphia Eagles. Travis's Chiefs won 38–35 in the first ever matchup between two brothers in a Super Bowl game.

Travis and Jason Kelce

Muhsin Muhammad

LEADING TACKLER

Safety Rodney Harrison played in four Super Bowls in his 15 years in the NFL with the San Diego Chargers and New England Patriots. He left the game as the Super Bowl's all-time leading tackler, with 34. Harrison's best Super Bowl performance came in Super Bowl XXXIX after the 2004 season. The safety notched 12 tackles, one pass breakup, one sack, and two interceptions. His Patriots defeated the Eagles 24–21.

A BIG HEAVE

Many legendary quarterbacks have played in the Super Bowl. But the longest pass play belongs to journeyman Jake Delhomme, who made only one appearance in the big game. In Super Bowl XXXVIII, the Carolina Panthers starter hit wide receiver Muhsin Muhammad for an 85-yard touchdown pass against the New England Patriots. The play broke the old mark of 81 yards. That play occurred in Super Bowl XXXI when the Green Bay Packers' Brett Favre connected with receiver Antonio Freeman.

WINNING AND LOSING

The Patriots became the first team to win six Super Bowls. They hit that mark when they defeated the Los Angeles Rams 13–3 in Super Bowl LIII after the 2018 season. But the season before, New England had lost its fifth Super Bowl. That tied a record set by the Denver Broncos in Super Bowl XLVIII in February 2014.

GLOSSARY

blitz
When a linebacker or a defensive back attacks the line of scrimmage to stop a run or sack the quarterback.

clutch
Performing well in an important situation that often decides a competition or game.

deflection
A tipped ball that changes direction.

franchise
A sports organization, including the top-level team and all minor league affiliates.

innovative
Having new ideas about how something can be done.

juke
A quick move used to get past a defender.

overtime
An extra period of play when the score is tied after regulation.

retirement
The end of one's career.

sack
A tackle of the quarterback behind the line of scrimmage before he can pass the ball.

safety
A score of two points for a team when its opponent is unable to advance the ball out of its own end zone.

scheme
A carefully designed plan.

special teams
The players on the field for kicking and punting plays.

stereotype
An oversimplified belief about someone or something.

MORE INFORMATION

Books

Graves, Will. *GOATs of Football*. Abdo, 2022.

Hanlon, Luke. *Football Video Games*. Abdo, 2025.

Stathes, Corbu. *Everything Football*. Abdo, 2025.

Online Resources

Booklinks
NONFICTION NETWORK
FREE! ONLINE NONFICTION RESOURCES

To learn more about Super Bowl record setters, please visit **abdobooklinks.com** or scan this QR code. These links are routinely monitored and updated to provide the most current information available.

INDEX

About the Author

David J. Clarke is a freelance sportswriter. Originally from Helena, Montana, he now lives in Savannah, Georgia.